FOUNDATIONS OF OUR NATION
DEVELOPING THE BILL OF RIGHTS

by Wil Mara

FOCUS
READERS

WWW.FOCUSREADERS.COM

Focus Readers is distributed by North Star Editions:
sales@northstareditions.com | 888-417-0195

Produced for Focus Readers by Red Line Editorial.

Content Consultant: Dr. Gideon Mailer, Associate Professor of History, University of Minnesota Duluth

Photographs ©: North Wind Picture Archives, cover, 1, 4–5, 7, 12–13, 15, 18–19, 21, 23, 26–27, 29; SuperStock/Glow Images, 9; Fine Art Images/Heritage Images/Glow Images, 11; gregobagel/iStockphoto, 25 (background); AleksandarNakic/iStockphoto, 25 (foreground)

ISBN
978-1-63517-244-7 (hardcover)
978-1-63517-309-3 (paperback)
978-1-63517-439-7 (ebook pdf)
978-1-63517-374-1 (hosted ebook)

Library of Congress Control Number: 2017935924

Printed in the United States of America
Mankato, MN
June, 2017

ABOUT THE AUTHOR

Wil Mara is the author of more than 200 books, many of which are educational titles for children. His interest in American history goes back to his childhood, spurred in part by a trip to Washington, DC, in the late 1970s during which he met President Jimmy Carter.

TABLE OF CONTENTS

CHAPTER 1

A NEW GOVERNMENT

The American Revolutionary War (1775–1783) was finally over. The United States was now an **independent** country. However, the US government had many problems. For example, it could not collect taxes from the states. The government had no way to get the money it needed.

British soldiers surrendered to the American army in 1781. A peace treaty was finished in 1783.

In 1787, many states sent **delegates** to a meeting in Philadelphia, Pennsylvania. Their job was to fix the problems with the government. The delegates had many debates. They decided to create a whole new type of government.

The delegates wrote the US Constitution. This document explained that the new government would have three branches. The legislative branch would create laws. It was known as Congress. The executive branch would make sure people followed the laws. This branch would be led by the president. The judicial branch would decide whether laws followed the Constitution.

The Constitution was written in Independence Hall in Philadelphia.

These three branches would make the government much stronger than it had been before. But not all of the delegates supported this idea. These delegates became known as Anti-Federalists.

They said the Constitution did not give people enough rights. They also believed the government would have too much power over the states.

Other delegates supported the Constitution. They were known as Federalists. These delegates believed the states could not handle issues that affected the whole country. For instance, a strong **federal** government would be better at dealing with foreign nations. The federal government could also solve disagreements between two or more states.

The Constitution was finished in September 1787. But the document would

Alexander Hamilton was one of the leaders of the Federalists.

not be official until nine states **ratified** it. Delegates knew this process would take months. People on both sides of the debate began writing articles. They wanted other citizens to understand their views.

HEATED DEBATES

The Federalists and Anti-Federalists had many heated debates. James Madison was a Federalist. He wrote, "If men were angels, no government would be necessary." He meant that people did not always do the right thing. For this reason, a strong government was necessary.

Samuel Bryan was an Anti-Federalist. He wrote, "One general government . . . would not be so **competent** to attend to various local concerns." He was saying that many problems are specific to a certain area. The people living in that area should decide how to solve those problems. The federal government should not be involved.

Robert Yates was another Anti-Federalist. "The judicial power of the United States will lean strongly in favor of the government," he wrote.

James Madison later became the president of the United States.

Yates feared that the judicial branch would want to spread its power wider and wider.

CHAPTER 2

THE MASSACHUSETTS COMPROMISE

In December 1787, three states ratified the Constitution. They were Delaware, Pennsylvania, and New Jersey. In January 1788, Georgia and Connecticut ratified the document, too. Only four more states were needed. Later that month, the leaders of Massachusetts held a meeting.

John Hancock was an Anti-Federalist leader from Massachusetts.

They had to decide whether their state would ratify the Constitution.

Many Anti-Federalists were at the meeting. They included John Hancock and Samuel Adams. These men did not want to ratify the Constitution in its current form. Instead, they suggested a **compromise**. Massachusetts would agree to ratify the document. However, the state would suggest **amendments**. After all, the Constitution allowed changes to be made. The amendments would limit the federal government's power. They would also describe the rights of the people and of the states. The Anti-Federalists expected

Samuel Adams later became the governor of Massachusetts.

these amendments to be made as soon as the new federal government went to work.

The vote in Massachusetts was close. But the state ratified the Constitution in February 1788. In other states, Anti-Federalist leaders took notice. They began asking for amendments, too.

In the spring of 1788, two more states ratified the Constitution. Only one more state was needed. In June 1788, New Hampshire became the ninth state. Similar to Massachusetts, it asked for amendments.

The Constitution was now official. But it was clear that many people wanted changes to the document. In March 1789, the new federal government met for the first time. Meanwhile, the Anti-Federalists were busy writing their amendments.

RATIFYING THE CONSTITUTION

	State	Date Ratified
1	Delaware	December 7, 1787
2	Pennsylvania	December 12, 1787
3	New Jersey	December 18, 1787
4	Georgia	January 2, 1788
5	Connecticut	January 9, 1788
6	Massachusetts	February 6, 1788
7	Maryland	April 28, 1788
8	South Carolina	May 23, 1788
9	New Hampshire	June 21, 1788
10	Virginia	June 25, 1788
11	New York	July 26, 1788
12	North Carolina	November 21, 1789
13	Rhode Island	May 29, 1790

CHAPTER 3

TWELVE ARTICLES

The first US Congress met in March 1789. One of the main issues was amending the Constitution. James Madison led these discussions. He made a list of several amendments.

The House of Representatives saw Madison's list first. After many debates, the House agreed on 17 amendments.

The first Congress met in New York City, which was the US capital from 1785 to 1790.

The amendments were sent to the Senate in August 1789. The Senate had more debates, and the list went down to 12. Each of the suggested amendments was known as an article.

The first two articles had to do with Congress. The first explained how many representatives would make up Congress. The second described rules for changing representatives' pay.

The other 10 articles had to do with the rights of citizens. The third article gave citizens the freedom of speech, press, and religion. This meant the government could not stop people from speaking their minds. People could even

The freedom of press allowed newspapers to print articles that were critical of leaders.

speak out against the government. Also, the government could not stop people from writing their opinions. In addition, the government could not interfere with people's religion. It could not favor one religion over another.

The fourth article gave people the right to own weapons. This right allowed people to defend themselves. It also let them organize **militias**. The fifth article said soldiers could not live in a citizen's house without permission. This had been a problem before the Revolutionary War.

The sixth article said government officials could not search a citizen's house without an order from a judge. The seventh said people do not have to **testify** against themselves during a trial. It also said a person cannot be tried twice for the same crime.

The eighth article gave people the right to a fair and speedy trial. The ninth article

The right to form militias was important to many Anti-Federalists.

said citizens have the right to a trial by **jury**. It also said the result of the trial could not be changed in a different court.

The tenth article said criminals could not receive cruel punishments.

The eleventh article said people had rights that were not mentioned in the Constitution. However, the article did not explain what these rights were. The twelfth article said any rights not given to the federal government were automatically the rights of the people and the states.

Both houses of Congress approved these 12 articles in September 1789. But the articles were not official yet. For that to happen, three-fourths of the states would have to ratify them.

THE NATIONAL ARCHIVES

The original 12 articles are on display at the National Archives Building in Washington, DC. This building also has copies of the Declaration of Independence and the Constitution.

CHAPTER 4

RATIFICATION

Each state debated the articles. Some states ratified all 12. But other states disliked the first two. Those two articles were not ratified by three-fourths of the states. As a result, they did not become amendments. The remaining 10 articles were ratified on December 15, 1791.

George Mason, a Virginia politician, strongly supported the articles.

These 10 amendments became known as the Bill of Rights.

The first article was never ratified. However, the second article was finally ratified in 1992. That was 202 years after Congress first approved it!

Many other amendments have been added over the years. One of the most important was the Thirteenth Amendment. It put an end to slavery in 1865. The Nineteenth Amendment was ratified in 1920. It gave women the right to vote.

The Constitution has been in effect for more than 225 years. One of the reasons for its success is that it can be

Representatives in Congress celebrated the Thirteenth Amendment in 1865.

changed. That was why the Bill of Rights became a part of the Constitution. People demanded a document that guaranteed their freedoms.

FOCUS ON
THE BILL OF RIGHTS

Write your answers on a separate piece of paper.

1. Write a letter to a friend explaining the main ideas of Chapter 2.

2. Do you think the right to own weapons is still important? Why or why not?

3. How many amendments did the Senate approve in 1789?

     A. 10
     B. 12
     C. 17

4. What might have happened if Hancock and Adams had not suggested the Massachusetts Compromise?

     A. The Bill of Rights would have been created sooner.
     B. The Constitution would not have been ratified.
     C. The Anti-Federalists would have lost power.

Answer key on page 32.

GLOSSARY

amendments
Official changes to a document.

competent
Able to do something.

compromise
An agreement in which both sides give up something they want.

delegates
People who speak on behalf of a larger group.

federal
Having to do with the top level of government.

independent
Able to make decisions without being controlled by another government.

jury
A group of ordinary citizens who decide a court case.

militias
Military forces formed by ordinary people trained to fight.

ratified
Gave something official approval.

testify
To speak in court.

TO LEARN MORE

BOOKS

Krull, Kathleen. *A Kid's Guide to America's Bill of Rights*. New York: Harper, 2015.

Lusted, Marcia Amidon. *The Bill of Rights*. Mankato, MN: The Child's World, 2016.

Schmidt, Maegan. *The US Constitution and Bill of Rights*. Minneapolis: Abdo Publishing, 2013.

NOTE TO EDUCATORS

Visit **www.focusreaders.com** to find lesson plans, activities, links, and other resources related to this title.

INDEX

Answer Key: 1. Answers will vary; **2.** Answers will vary; **3.** B; **4.** B